so my mother,
she lives in the clouds

and other stories

christopher d. dicicco

AVAILABLE WHEREVER BOOKS ARE SOLD.

HYPERTROPHIC PRESS
P.O. Box 423 New Market, AL 35761
www.hypertrophicpress.com

HYPERTROPHIC LITERARY
Summer 2018

Editor-in-Chief: Lynsey Morandin
Creative Director: Jeremy Bronaugh
Aquisitions Editor: Madeline Anthes

Featured Artist: Veronika Vajdova

Hypertrophic Literary is published quarterly by Hypertrophic Press. Past and current issues can be purchased online at Amazon.com. Submissions are read throughout the year. For complete submission guidelines, please visit hypertrophicpress.com. For advertising rates and inquiries, please email hypertrophicliterary@gmail.com or view the website. No portion of Hypertrophic Literary may be reproduced without permission. All rights reserved. Hypertrophic Literary honors other cultures and maintains the local spelling of each contributor.

P.O. Box 423
New Market, AL
35761

www.hypertrophicpress.com

Hypertrophy [hahy-pur-truh-fee]: excessive growth or accumulation of any kind

HYPERTROPHIC LITERARY
CALL FOR SUBMISSIONS

FICTION. POETRY. ART.

We're always looking for content for our upcoming issues. Whether you write or make art, we want passion, pieces that make us feel something: *elation, fear, desperation* – *whatever*. We're looking for literary work that goes beyond everyday experience and delves deep into the emotions that drive us. Our goal is to make reading not only a psychological experience, but a physical one too.

SUBMISSION GUIDELINES:

You may submit up to three (3) stories <u>or</u> ten (10) poems at once. Artists may submit a representative sample or portfolio of their artwork with no less than twenty (20) images.

Simultaneous submissions are accepted.

Responses can take up to three months.
2-week fast track responses available for $5
HYPERTROPHICPRESS.BIGCARTEL.COM

Please visit our website for full submission guidelines before you email your submission to
HYPERTROPHICLITERARY@GMAIL.COM

FEATURING:

TOMMY DEAN / ROBERT JAMES RUSSELL

NICK ALTI / MONICA MACANSANTOS

KRISTEN M. PLOETZ / JENNIFER FLISS

KATHRYN LIPARI / HALEY CAMPBELL

FRANCIS DAULERIO / ELISABETH ALAIN

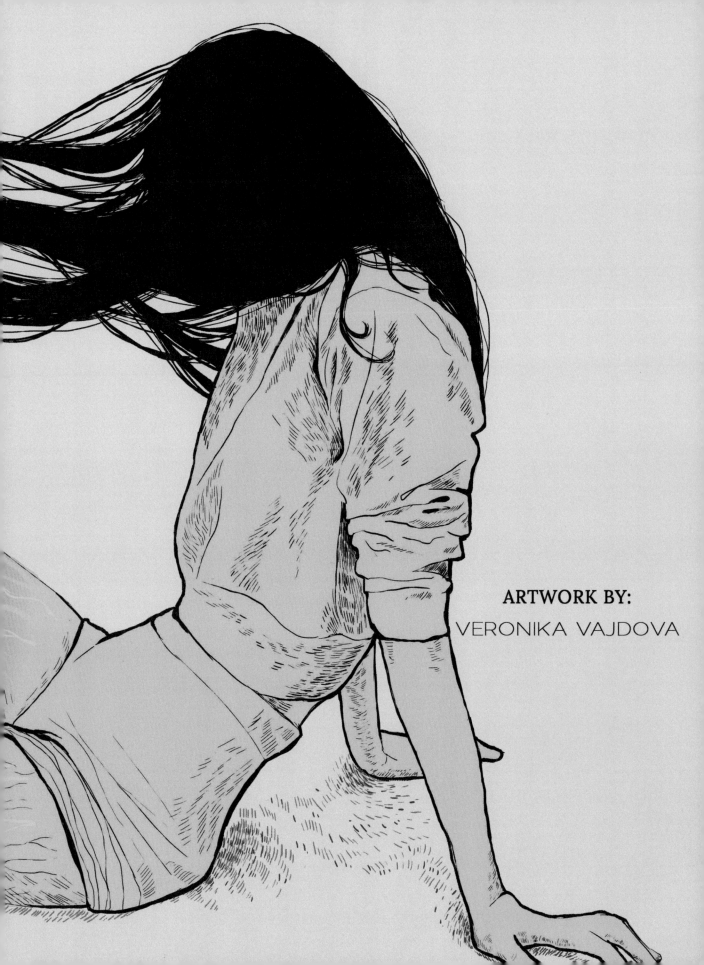

ARTWORK BY:

VERONIKA VAJDOVA

YOUR MOTHER HAS ANOTHER BLACK EYE AND

Kathryn Lipari

You cannot find a word in the dictionary or thesaurus
for the emotion that skitters on sharp little claws from your bowels to your lungs

You relive the night you blackened her eye
you were fourteen and drunk, she forty and drunker

You imagine your nine-year-old son at her house every Monday afternoon
confused by her tipsy, scared by her drunk

You recollect previous black eyes and the causes she attributed them to
a spider bite, a burnt out light bulb, slippery shoes

You try not to remember her accompanying injuries
bruises on her skinny forearms, bloated ankle, blood clotted at her hairline

You remind yourself that she has been sober for four years
You remind yourself that she *says* she has been sober for four years

You search her kitchen
open the green plastic bottle of Schweppes Ginger Ale and sniff

You remember how it felt when you were certain she was drinking herself to death

You resolve to call her every evening and tell her you love her
You make yourself an oversized martini at precisely five o'clock
You yell at her for taking your kids out to ice cream, then giving them soda at dinner
You fail to imagine yourself alive when she is dead

You stop yourself from reaching up to stroke the yellowing
purple crescent under her green eye

You picture your daughters old, alone, drinking nightly

You do everything but what you truly want to—
cradle her in your arms like a child and howl

LEMON SCENT

Elisabeth Alain

My mother is grieving again. I know because our bathroom has been sparkling clean every single day this week. Not so much as a stray eyelash on the side of the sink. The synthetic lemon scent stings the back of my throat as I watch her, elbow-deep in denial, scrubbing the toilet bowl, removing every last trace of something only she can see. Emerging, all blotched cheeks and puffy eyes, she announces, "These chemicals, they irritate me; I've always been sensitive." My younger sisters dart between bedrooms, lost in a made-up world, barely registering the excuse, let alone questioning it. I've seen her though, bent over in convulsing sobs, leaning hard on the side of the bath for support.

This merciless cleaning will continue for days, my mother dropping often to her knees to spot-clean an already spotless floor. Then she will gather us all at the kitchen table for dinner. This my sisters will notice, and they will protest loudly at not being able to eat in front of the TV. She will beguile us with platitudes of how lucky we are to have each other, us four, all girls together, how lovely this house is compared to the last place, slipping in that our latest step dad has moved out. Later on I'll hear her telling Nana on the phone how well we've taken it, agree that we're such resilient girls and that we'll all be fine in a few weeks. She won't hear my sisters telling each other how they'll miss the piggy backs up and down the stairs or how they bet they won't get to go swimming on the holidays anymore. She won't hear the click of my bedside lamp being turned back on after she's gone to bed, or know that I'm still awake, listening out for burglars and imagining house fires.

When my mother left our father, she cleaned the bathroom of the new flat twice a day for months, taking a toothbrush to the plugholes, flicking out black gunge onto white tiles. She polished the rust-spotted mirror with a vinegar-doused cloth, buffing in squeaky circles, searching through blinked tears for a perfect reflection.

Dad makes us clean his bathroom on our weekend visits, inspecting afterwards all four taps and the underside of the sink to make sure we've done it just right. My sisters get sent to bed early if he finds a soap stain on the cabinet or if there's any dust gathered in the corners of the floor. I get to stay up late to cook the "grown-up dinner" and refill his dwindling drink while he watches TV. He plays with my hair and tells me, "You're a good girl, not like your mother."

When he starts to fall asleep, I'll wriggle my aching shoulder from under the weight of his arm and get up off the sofa. "Where you goin', angel?" he'll mutter, the vodka smoothing the sharpness that usually edges his voice.

"Bathroom", I'll say.

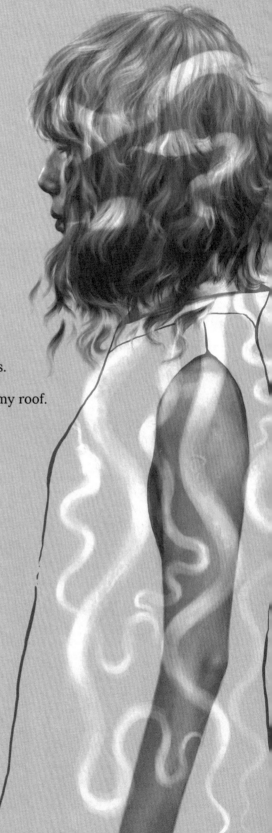

LIGHTMARE

Nick Alti

On my roof with him
you watch Northern Lights pulse beautiful, beautiful
while I, Fuseli's mangled dreamwork
hunt an earwig in the attic.
I am now Lord Pale Nightwalker;
every light shown on me reveals a nightmare.

Never think of me as a miracle—those are beneficial anomalies.
Are you as sad as you look?
you asked before you climbed the utility pole, hand in his, to my roof.
To pretend it was me instead, I undress
in this parasitic crawlspace. I'm a conflagration
driving things that have hearts
far away from me.

I hear you together above me.
He fills you like a wound healing.

I eat no savior's flesh,
drink no good man's blood. I'm learning
how to distinguish field mice by the shape of their ears
as he learns the freckles of your thighs,
lips upon constellations.

No great light shines through the warm space
between his hand & your hip, his tongue
& your clit.

Is this your famous kiss?

I exist as a spear-ridden mastodon nearing a cliff; I crave
to feel like weather—
everywhere & genuine.

11

A MAN WHO HELPS THE NEIGHBORS

Jennifer Fliss

The crow tilts its head and looks at me with his onyx eye saying, yeah, you saw it too, I know. I know you want to say, says the crow, oh he was just helping with the plumbing under her kitchen sink, patching up her siding. Her siding is what got you into this trouble in the first place. In the first place it was Celeste and she was the landlady and she was all, to tell you the truth, I am just useless without a man. A man who, when you got married, everyone said was worth his weight in gold or at least in Microsoft stock because it was 2009 and that was a thing that meant you had great value and, anyway, he didn't have a stock portfolio and neither did you. Did you think that wouldn't matter because you had love? Love, as you now know, is for chumps and now you think it might be time to go, but you won't admit it to anyone else because he's just cleaning her gutters – it's so hard for her to reach those places. Those places where a woman can't reach but, oh sure a man can, a man certainly can reach those spots hard to get to. Get to the point, he says when you're talking. When you're talking he rolls his eyes like the most delicate of teenagers. Teenagers like you used to be, years ago when you hung out by the p-patch outside the high school with him. With him, you smoked cloves and nibbled on chard you both were too proud to say was bitter and, when the season was right, you ate not-yet-ready blackberries and talked about how obviously no one told these gardeners that blackberries

were a weed and, if allowed, it would grow and grow and take over with its tart juicy berries and its sharp as fuck thorns that got caught in your hair and drew blood from your skin. Your skin. Your skin was so young, dewy, elastic, soft – the skin of a child. A child neither one of you wanted. You wanted it, but you didn't say. Didn't say so since you both decided no, no children. No children in this house. This house is mine, he said. He said, I paid for it and I don't want any kids mucking it up and this is what we wanted, right? Right now, you realized you changed your mind about the baby and then you wouldn't, couldn't get over the miscarriage and he was like, you just fucking mope around the house and burn chocolate chip cookies like you're Betty fucking Crocker's fucked up sister and that is why I went to Laura. Laura said its time for you to get over it. It's funny to hear advice on a dead baby from the woman fucking your husband. Your husband is surprised when you carry three suitcases and a duffel bag out to the car. The car is yours, you tell him. Tell him you're leaving him and also point out that Laura's house is brick and doesn't have siding and I don't know anymore who you are. You are not at all clear on who I am. I am not for you. You are, he said. He said he loved my thighs and my fiery road rage and the way I ate the frosting off cake first. First, there was love.

Love, you said.

You said, *calm down.*

HERITABLE
Haley Campbell

we can talk about
pain all you want

we can address
my body filled with

pins, or sharp slivers
of glass (picked up

where? The kitchen floor?
Did someone

drop a jar before I moved,
leaving me

a few skittered pieces
on the tile?)
            we can talk

about mothers, about
wombs, barriers of blood

however you conceive
the soul, what ferries hurt

from body to body across
generations, electric

arcs searing from brain
to brain
            we can talk

about inheritance,
which is to press

responsibility into
another's body

and expecting other limbs
to bear its weight

14

MY SYLLABLES

Jennifer Fliss

When you say I'm sorry I can't pronounce this and look directly at me, I just say "present" and think I am giving you a gift. It is as if you think I am poisoning your mouth with my syllables. Your smile isn't apologetic, but the smile of a middle-aged teacher living two hours from the nearest Applebee's.

You scroll through the class names and not once do you stutter or stub your tongue on anyone else's name. This goes on every day. Allen, Barker, Smith, White. You eventually just skip over mine, look for me and nod when it's my name's turn.

Later, when you push that stubbed tongue down my throat, you still say nothing and I ask why not and you point at your mouth as if to say, I'm chewing right now and I'll answer you once I swallow. I am not a rude guy, you seem to be saying.

The janitors' closet is filled with all kinds of things. Not just bleach and mops and Playboys.

When you say all the girls like this, I say what girls, because where I come from – down the block – none of the girls would like this. We've talked about it – you – at the top of the slide where we apologize to the little kids but don't move. We only talked about it before and we all agree that there's no way we would even. Now I barely go to the playground. It's for kids. But I can hear laughter echo from the top of the enclosed slide when I walk home. Sometimes I cross the street to avoid hearing that sound.

When you say it's our little secret, it's really not little. It's everything I can think of. It's melted solder in my veins trying to piece me together again because maybe then I'd shine and you could see me. And here, I made you something in art class. It's my stained glass heart. You say it's pretty.

I want to talk to you about the smiley face you scribbled next to the B minus on my essay. Do you really think I don't understand what it's like to be a cockroach? I know what it feels like to be underfoot, an unwanted pest who skitters at the very hint of light. I know these creatures. They share the peeling linoleum and late-night brawls and empty vodka bottles with me and my mom.

When I tell you about it, you tell me I'm safe here. With you. In this closet. With all the poison. I start to wonder what "safe" means and you take my face in your hands and I think I might know.

One day after class, you etch your initials into my desk like a sixth-grade wannabe bad boy. As I walk out, my fingers brush another desk and find the splinters of your name. I check the desk next to it. And the one next to that. And the one next to that. I stay late to check and all the desks in all the rooms are branded by you, as if you own us all.

When you say if I tell, and pantomime a gun, your thumb the trigger, I wonder why. You said you loved me. Even though you don't say my name.

SOLITUDE AUDIBLE

Nick Alti

Never has night been so alive as the inaugural hour
of your new alone.

Instructions for planting a hyacinth:
get a shovel from any unlocked shed
eat dirt
stop it, stop eating all this dirt
nowhere left for the hyacinth
eat your famine-worthy dirt, feel meaningful if possible.

Coyotes in nearby wild howling
frightening you howling
to summon homeward what's been lost. Tear apart a tomcat
to face no moment quiet. Away from moon
two comets weep Zion wide open.

You'll need hear only once
I don't know how long I can love you
to agree. Afterwards,
you'll maintain yourself in the way a starling
hijacks a robin's nest; how an ocean
vomits intestines of an elephant seal ravaged by the jaws of a shark.

In each picture you've collected—embarrassed for being sentimental—you'll discover
traces of sadness on every face no matter what background foliage blossoms.
One thing lighting doesn't change is that you're awful.

Those comets you beg to pause in sky
dissipate into living night
leaving you to truly confront entropy;
never in astronomy have you more than this desired pity.

Lone coyote can't sleep amidst such audible hopelessness; so loud are the leaves curling up,
wanting for rain.

Something (bird?) near the concord vineyard
has been screaming every day. Not cawing, no normal warbles.
Within this birdish thing   there's agony.
You wonder when you'll start to grow feathers.

A THRUMMING SILENCE

Tommy Dean Previously published in *JMWW*

The day my brother died, I broke into my best friend's house. I skipped school that day, feigning a stomach ache. My mother, a light sleeper, plagued by anxiety that hovered over her only at night like a muslin sheet, assumed that the constant flushing toilet coming from my bathroom was evidence of my flu-like symptoms. This ruse wasn't my favorite way to fake sickness, but it was effective, and then I'd have the house to myself for four uninterrupted hours.

I must have heard the sirens, the entire town erupting in wailing chaos, but we never assume the emergency has anything to do with us. Our minds quickly account for the whereabouts of our family members, ticking off their usual placements stuck in their settings like characters in a book. My mother was sitting behind her desk, typing in numbers, balancing accounts; my father was at the elementary school teaching science; and my brother was at the high school, tipped back in his chair, math quiz finished quickly, telling jokes that even his teachers laughed at despite their warnings of detention if he didn't shut up.

I didn't exactly break into Ryan's house. I knew about the hide-a-key, how obviously fake the rock looked, a specked mica among dull gray stones delivered one spring break when we were eight and were still excited by the loud rush of falling rocks from the bed of a dump truck. Turning the key, I wasn't afraid. There wasn't an alarm or even a dog, but just the thrumming silence of appliances. There was mystery among the familiar. I'd been in the house countless times, but never alone.

A week later, the police told us while we sat on the couch, the May sun streaming in through the window behind us, that witness accounts placed my brother on county road 350 East driving at reckless speeds. "What's a reckless speed to a couple of grannies and an old farmer?" I ask the middle-aged cop, whose gray chest hair I could see through the bulge between the buttons of his uniform shirt. Officer Fugit shook his head while my dad escorted me to my room. He settled me on my bed, the comforter cold, his hand on my shoulder sweltering.

"We're all in pain, Dylan. Your mother, she can't handle these kinds of questions."

"You-" I started, but the haunting was already behind his eyes. "Then we shouldn't expect any answers."

Most kids would brag about looking at their best friend's sister's underwear or drinking the father's liquor or unearthing the unlocked but holstered handgun in the mother's nightstand. But you know where they found me? In Ryan's old playroom, vintage toys scattered around me – Transformers, Ninja Turtles, He-Man, and G.I. Joe – arranged in an epic battle, a storyline I didn't want to give up as my mother stood over me, breath ragged as a balloon that's come untied. Her wrists, draped across my shoulders, twitching from the mechanical motion of typing. I held up a Ninja Turtle, the red-masked one, and asked, "Do you remember this?"

Later, after we were sure that Ryan's parents wouldn't press charges, after Ryan had cussed at me and ignored me, after we had moved a hundred miles away, my mom on disability for carpal tunnel, and my dad finding a job as an assistant principal, after the rumors of there being another car, the image of black paint streaked across the bumper of my brother's car, after the town sent it off to the county dump and it had been recycled and turned into sheet metal riveted to someone's roof, after I had finished middle school, after my brother's voice had faded to a single word, "Dude," repeating throughout our new house, I got a package in the mail, no sender identified, but the address familiar. I opened it cautiously in my room, this new house only having two bedrooms to keep the ghosts out, to find a set of Transformers, carefully packed in bubble wrap, the plasticized colors vibrant and unmarked. I placed them on my desk, mechanical arms outstretched, frozen in battle, waiting for someone to notice.

FIELD OF MALACHITE

Haley Campbell

Today you come home to find
your lover in pieces: a thigh

limp in the front hall, one foot
balanced precariously on the sink,

shoulders poking out behind the couch,
hands nowhere to be seen. You collect

everything you can, draw your lover together
with what gentleness you have to spare.

You're used to this by now. Outside
the sky gloams green, quiet and troubling.

You find your lover's hair and smooth it down,
adjust a scapula and offer reassurance

that reeds and riverbanks are temporary, tangible
only as long as the sky keeps a color

or bodies keep souls. In the morning,
on the pillow, you find your lover's hands.

BITTER PILLS

Kristen M. Ploetz

By the time Minah and Pet arrived at Eradication Partners, LLP, they'd already completed the easy part of splitting their marital assets. To each: six silver-plated demitasse spoons (though they were both tea drinkers, the only thing left in common by the end), four juice glasses (enough for impromptu brunches in temporary apartments during the rebound phase), two sets of queen sheets (Pet ran cold and took the flannel; Minah, the Percale – her core temp, like her baseline impatience, was fueled by nuclear fission), one Dachshund, one hunter green Adirondack chair (their monogram on the front seat slats to be sanded smooth at a later date), and five albums by The Clash.

When things were indivisible, they haggled like weary buyers and sellers on a hot day at the flea. Tears were shed. Feelings were hurt. Minah got the camera (it helped that the photographic record of their twelve-year marriage lacked evidence of her existence except for two honeymoon photos and that time at Jason's BBQ last August). Pet got the vintage Weber (he liked grilled peaches but she couldn't stomach anything charred, including the indelible marks left by "The Vulture" on the carrion of their marriage). Five forks and four knives for her, four forks and five knives for him (they only let their guards down to laugh when they remembered what happened to the tenth setting). They donated the yellow canoe to the boys' camp across the pond but each kept an oar as some kind of metaphoric reminder of their breakdown.

But since they couldn't agree on how to cleave the memories of their sex life – what to keep, what to share, what to burn down – the judge ordered them to consult with Eradication Partners. How else to divide the exhilaration of firsts (like the time on their new kitchen table or in the neighbors' pool or when they got too drunk with Rae and Brandon while camping)? How else to tear along the perforated line of learned preferences (harder in the middle of the month) and erogenous zones (the inside of her thigh, the top curve of his right ear) and ways to make each other scream (blindfolds and dirty words nobody thought they'd know)? And so it was that they were forced to yield to the compound pharmacy of Eradication Partners where the laws of passion could be distilled down into an easy to swallow pill that would erase all they knew. It was better this way, they agreed.

Minah arrived first, Pet ten minutes later. She held the door for him, and he pulled out her chair. On the table, two blue pills, two glasses of water, and two paper napkins.

Toast.

Swallow.

Wipe.

Hug.

Minah left first, Pet two minutes later. As he passed through the door, he tongued the pill still inside his cheek and saw Minah's napkin at the bottom of the wastebasket, a tiny arc of blue peeking out from the fold.

POEM FOR A SICK CHILD ON THE FOURTH OF JULY

Francis Daulerio

Night again,
and the two of us rocking,
both wanting sleep,
while the neighboring farm blows off
the last of its mortars,
my hands still smelling of hose water
and Pink Brandywine leaves.

A small plastic giraffe
with big green eyes
and a pair of blue overalls
is digging
its outstretched arm into my hip
from its misplaced home
between the cushions of our glider.

Outside, as the celebration dims,
the night resigns itself again
to darkness, and your gut-sick body
finally slacks into mine.

        Yes,
you love me now
because, when your mother sleeps,
I am left of what you know,
        and yes,
in tomorrow's tired daylight
I will likely hide this toy giraffe
somewhere far from you and this chair
that has, tonight, assumed itself
our cradle.

For now, though, I will
breathe you in,
commit your tiny form to memory,
and stay here,
uncomfortable like this,
for as long as you will let me,
knowing how quickly time takes us
away from who we've been.

YOU SAID I WANT

Haley Campbell

you said *I want*
to want what you want

you want this quiver-toothed
sugar-sick ache, gifts unopened before a birthday,
before learning everything underneath the paper
isn't beautiful. *I want to want*

what you want I want
three years to simmer in Texas heat a thousand
five hundred miles from your cologne I want
pause buttons sewn to the seams of my dresses
want every night to whisper you, want
strangers bleaching you out of my body

I want to want your hands tumbling toward my flesh
your hands hovering over
a child's round head I want not
the child, not the humming order
of my mind in such sharp discord with your
kickdrum neurons, want you suited
salaried stable
stale, want to want you here
now whole and unvarnished

I want
　　　　to want
　　　　　　　　the asphalt lot

the place you touched me last

　　　　　　　　　　　　want

the two of us sustained in that same
sugared ache, and wanting
for nothing

24

STOPOVER

Monica Macansantos   Previously published in *Five Quarterly*

When Cathy's plane began its descent into Austin, Texas, she lifted the shade of her window and peered outside. From where she sat, the city streets trickled from the downtown area to the sparsely populated fringes of the dustbowl below. A vein of water wound its way through the city grid, appearing and disappearing as the base of her window bobbed up and down beside her. As the plane tilted to its left side, a bell tower emerged into view, and the trees and brick buildings that surrounded it seemed to reinforce its genteel authority. She imagined Evangeline biking to class under those trees, her wavy hair streaming behind her, the way it did in those tin-framed, open-air jeepneys they rode together to class in their sprawling college campus in Manila.

She and Evangeline had both been English majors in college, and when they graduated Evangeline took a teaching job at an agricultural college near the foothills of Mount Makiling while Cathy left the Philippines with her family to begin a new life in the suburbs of San Francisco. She wasn't even "Cathy" back when Evangeline knew her, and when Evangeline called her by the name "Katrina" on the phone, she felt her old life tightening around her like an ill-fitting dress she had outgrown. She hadn't intentionally cast away her old name or her memories of the old country during her three years in America. Like scales she had shed, she had hardly been aware that some of her old habits had fallen away from her repertoire.

This wasn't her hometown, but as she walked up the tarmac and into the small, glass-paneled airport she felt as though this were a sort of homecoming and she pictured Evangeline being awed by her accent as well as the ease with which she dealt with Americans. She hadn't been back to the old country since she had left, and this was the next best thing to coming home – meeting a character of her past whom she could overwhelm with her knowledge of America.

One of the fringe benefits she enjoyed as a check-in girl for American Airlines were free flights to any town with an airport in the United States. She took advantage of this to explore her adopted country, and she posted pictures of her trips to New York and the other big cities on Facebook religiously. She followed every like, every admiring remark about her success in this land that everyone back home called "the land of the free." It came to the point that she needed to get on a plane to hear their comments in her head, for only by doing this could she remind herself of the freedom she now possessed.

When Evangeline messaged her telling her that she was moving to Austin, Texas, for graduate school, Cathy looked forward to having a couch to sleep on in a town she had only read about in in-flight magazines. Evangeline was probably as bewildered as she had been when she first arrived in America, but Cathy was sure she was smart enough to navigate the town or at least to know how to buy a couch from a local thrift store. Cathy could take care of the other parts of this trip like coaxing Evangeline to a bar or teaching her how to flirt with American boys.

Plane just landed, Cathy typed into her phone, her boot heels neatly clicking against the grooves of the airport escalator. *You can pick me up now.*

All right. I texted you my address. You can rent a car or take a shuttle to my place, Evangeline replied.

What? You don't have a car? Cathy texted back, alarmed.

I said so in my email. Car rental companies near the exit. Sorry, was Evangeline's reply.

Sighing, Cathy pushed her phone into her jeans pocket and made her way through the crowd of families, students, and returning servicemen in khaki boots and camouflage uniforms who stepped aside as she passed without making eye contact with her. She felt as though she were walking through a forest of towering bodies that were too indifferent to do her harm. She approached the Avis counter and fell in line right behind a family of Indians and a bespectacled old man in a gray suit who carried a battered leather briefcase. The crowd that had gathered around the baggage carousels thinned out, and she watched on as families in summer clothing entered the airport and let out excited screams when spotting their uniformed sons who lumbered towards them. Her friend was too poor to extend the same welcome to her, and when the uniformed teenager behind the Avis counter handed her a bill, she realized she didn't have enough money saved up for this trip to be as mobile as she wanted to be.

Upon Evangeline's suggestion, she reserved a seat on an airport shuttle and she shared a ride with a quiet Asian girl who peered near-sightedly into her iPhone and two middle-aged women in jeans and t-shirts who chattered about a bridal shower as they clasped their newly bought cowboy hats to their bellies. The houses they passed on their way to the city were just as seedy as the one-storey, clapboard bungalows that surrounded her apartment building on the outskirts of San Francisco. Outside her shuttle window, mothers pushed strollers across the street as small children grasped the hems of their worn, thrift store skirts while men in baseball caps and baggy pants walked by the roadside, ignoring vehicles that barreled past them. A twin-sized mattress and box spring peeked from the mouth of a dumpster that faced the road, and she remembered the futon mattress she and her boyfriend had retrieved outside a vacant lot near her apartment building just months before. It creaked under them during their make-out sessions and her boyfriend complained that it was giving him back problems whenever he slept over, but the two hundred dollars she had saved was enough to pay for a two-night stay at an airport hotel in one of those sleepy Midwestern towns whose name she didn't bother to remember. Money passed through her fingers like water, and again she was back to scrimping. The shuttle that bore her to her friend's apartment was like a sealed capsule with its windows rolled up, shielding its passengers from the grayness that spread itself before them like the stale pages of an unread book.

After skirting past the university and entering a quieter neighborhood of oak trees and clapboard houses nestled behind flower bushes and evenly mown lawns, the shuttle pulled into a parking space in front of a gray, benign-looking apartment building with arched entrances and a pair of curved staircases that wound their way from a raised platform on the first floor to the right and left sides of the second floor. She dialed Evangeline's number and a door on the second floor opened. Evangeline stepped outside holding her phone to her ear, and when she spotted Cathy at the foot of the stairs leading to her floor she flipped her phone shut, smiled, and waved.

In America, Cathy had learned the habit of spreading her arms as a friend approached, and Evangeline whispered "I missed you so much!" into her ear as they hugged. The touch of Evangeline's palm against her back awakened memories of long ago when Evangeline brushed Cathy's arm teasingly whenever Cathy asked her to explain Derrida's definition of différance to her, as though gleefully surprised that anyone she considered her friend could find such easy concepts so difficult to understand. Evangeline never lacked friends despite spending hours in the library, and when she did socialize with the likes of Cathy, it was with a lighthearted friendliness that she guarded her secrets of success. She was a favorite of the professors, a perpetual guardian and dispenser of answers when no one else in the classroom was bright enough to follow a professor's train of thought.

The tidiness with which Evangeline conducted her own life befuddled Cathy: she had left her hometown in the northern provinces to study in Manila, locked herself up in her dorm room to study, and, despite her shyness with boys, had defied her classmates' expectations by dating the president of the student government. Her life, it seemed, had been carefully planned out; even two years of teaching in a sleepy agricultural town south of Manila seemed to have gotten her places.

Evangeline grasped her shoulders, pulled back, and inspected her. "You've gained weight!" she said in Tagalog. Cathy was sure she would've felt insulted if Evangeline said the same thing in English, but in their native tongue it was a common greeting. Evangeline knew just how to tell a friend the embarrassing truth.

"At least I'm gaining some weight. You've remained a stick since we graduated," she said.

"You know me. I jog every day for lack of a vice," Evangeline said, letting go of Cathy's shoulders. "I made adobo for dinner, by the way. My dad's version." She turned and led Cathy upstairs.

"Great. That's one less meal to spend for," Cathy said, pulling at the straps of her backpack.

"This country's crazy. You have to swipe your card for every move you make. That's what I miss about the Philippines."

"I know. Back home you can laze around and expect a relative to send you money from abroad."

Evangeline turned and gave Cathy a hard look of reproach.

"Well, not everybody," Cathy said, forcing a smile.

Evangeline's face softened. Cathy was amused by her friend's sternness, a habit acquired, Cathy joked to herself, from having to deal with minds that weren't as sharp as hers.

"I see what you mean. My aunt thinks I'm making enough to save up for a house back home. If ever she knew how expensive it is to live here..." They had reached the door of her apartment, and Evangeline turned the knob, pushed it open, and stood aside to let Cathy pass.

"My futon was delivered a week ago. Just in time for your visit."

Cathy spotted the black futon pushed to the right side of the living room behind a chocolate brown coffee table with a growing stack of magazines. The entire living room was bathed in the afternoon sunlight that shone through the room's floor-to-ceiling window. Cathy would've been hesitant to sign a lease for an apartment with such a large window, but when one lived in such gentrified surroundings, one's instincts weren't sharpened by the constant threat of break-ins. She felt a pang of envy as she paced around the apartment and spotted a large, hardwood desk beside the futon couch and a bookcase pushed against the wall that marked the end of the living room. It would've been the perfect writing space for her: a room with a view, offering enough space for her mind to wander.

She took off her backpack, set it down on the floor, and approached Evangeline's desk. "This is a beautiful desk," she said, running her fingers along its varnished surface and closing her eyes.

"Forty dollars from a poet who was moving to Chicago," Evangeline said, leaning against the wall dividing the living room from the kitchen. "It's cherry-wood."

"I wouldn't even have made the distinction," Cathy said.

"Poetry used to be written at that desk. It's a desk meant for you, not for me," Evangeline said, and she laughed as though wanting to ease Cathy back into the past, back into the ill-fitting dress.

"I just have enough space in my apartment for a futon and a coffee table," Cathy said, sinking into the futon and pulling her backpack towards her feet.

"So your coffee table doubles as your writing desk?" Evangeline asked.

"As a reading desk, it does." Cathy unzipped her backpack and peered into it, feeling Evangeline's eyes following every twitch on her face.

"I miss reading your stories," Evangeline said, retreating behind the kitchen wall.

Cathy pulled out from her backpack the library books she had brought with her and set them on the coffee table. Both were due in two weeks: H.P. Lovecraft's *The Dunwich Horror* and Nicole Krauss's *The History of Love*. It was an odd pairing, but there was no need for her to follow any syllabus or thematic grouping now that she was out of school. She was educating herself, not enslaving herself to any institution or order.

The smell of soy sauce and bay leaves wafted into the living room and a wave of memories washed away the antiseptic calmness of the present, revealing the comforting confusion of her past. She was in her grandmother's house in the old country, sitting on a bamboo bench as her grandmother puttered about in her stone kitchen. Her grandmother's *adobo* smelled sweeter, more acrid. America, back then, stood for everything her adulthood meant to her: an unrealized vastness into which her parents, after getting their visa petitions approved, would initiate her. She was in college by this time and she was telling her grandmother, who was ladling the pork and chicken stew into a bowl, that she wanted to be a writer, maybe a journalist. "But before you leave, you should learn how to cook our food," her grandmother said, setting down the bowl on a linoleum-covered bamboo table and inviting her to eat. "In America, you'll have food on the table all the time. But unless you learn how to cook our food, you'll never be able to feed that belly."

The first *adobo* she made when she had moved out of her parents' house was too bland to awaken memories of her grandmother's cooking. She gave up

on her first try, and now subsisted on a diet of TV dinners and canned chili. As long as she kept her stomach filled she could keep her longing for the past at bay. A more skilled cook like Evangeline, on the other hand, could afford to be oblivious to the longings she awakened in her friend.

> ## " If words fractured a friendship, alcohol healed it. "

"You must be thirsty. Would you like some tea?" Evangeline asked, emerging from the kitchen with a wooden spoon in her hand.

"Do you have beer in your fridge?" Cathy placed *The History of Love* on her lap and opened it to a random page.

"Oh, I don't keep alcohol in my house."

Evangeline's cheerfulness only served to fan her disappointment.

"For real?"

"I just can't drink alone."

"The only liquids I drink are alcohol. And water."

"I'll get you a glass of water then." Evangeline disappeared behind the wall, opened her fridge and cupboards, and reemerged with a glass of cold water. Placing the glass on the coffee table, she looked at the book in Cathy's lap and asked, "What are you reading?"

"*The History of Love*. I was just looking at a random page. Haven't really started yet."

"Oh, that's such a good book," Evangeline said. Then, straightening herself, she said, "I'd like to see one of your stories in print someday."

"That wouldn't happen." Cathy bit her lip.

"Sure it will. This is America."

"I don't have time to write these days," Cathy said, snapping her book shut and returning it to the coffee table. "There are just too many good books to read."

"Don't you remember Dr. Cruz comparing my failed attempts at writing with your polished prose?" Evangeline was behaving like a mother this time, and it seemed as though she took joy in dispensing kindness to her less fortunate friend.

"Why write if there are so many good books to read?" Cathy asked.

"I don't know. You were just so good at it. I still remember that story you wrote about two blind men."

"I've been doing some living too, you know." For how could she justify her own laziness to Evangeline? Life rolled on whether Cathy liked it or not, and she had other pressing concerns to deal with like rent, bills, and coworker ex-boyfriends who nagged her with handwritten letters filled with misspellings and grammatical errors. She didn't see any reason to be choosy; it was bad enough that her coworkers had turned her bookishness into a running joke, and she chose to laugh along with them rather than alienate her new friends. After all, it was the ones who had never been to college who treated her as though she were one of them – the college-educated among them behaved as though they were too good to be hauling suitcases onto conveyor belts and working alongside new immigrants like her. Traveling allowed her to forget the less savory details of her life, but the sheets of stationery she left blank on the writing desks in the rooms where she slept reminded her of a larger emptiness she preferred not to face.

Evangeline withdrew again behind the kitchen wall and reemerged after a few minutes with a bowl of steaming hot *adobo* which she set on the dining table. Like Cathy's grandmother, Evangeline nodded at her and said, "There's no pork in here, just lean, skinless chicken breasts. I also made salad."

> " She wanted to see something different in this town, something that would astonish her. "

On the table, she set two embroidered placemats on which she placed two matching floral plates. Cathy sometimes suspected that Evangeline's orderliness was a tic meant to disguise a hidden chaos. But Evangeline executed these gestures with so much ease, as though this weren't a mask but the foundation on which her life had been built. It seemed at this point in their friendship that Cathy had to give her friend a cleaner justification of her failure to accomplish her goals, since cleanliness seemed to be the only language Evangeline was capable of comprehending.

Cathy suspected that Evangeline saw life as a series of signposts pointing one to a sought goal, and that every wrong turn one made was the result of one's own miscalculations. Over dinner, she told Evangeline that she had sent her resume to fifty newspapers upon arriving in America and that only one of them asked her for a writing sample, after which she was informed that the position for which she applied had been filled.

"Then you could've applied to fifty more places," Evangeline said, as though her mind were immune to reason.

"Vangie, you don't get it, do you? I needed a job. I couldn't get one at a newspaper. Americans don't like our English." This conversation was exhausting her, and she leaned back in her chair and pushed away her food.

"That's not true. Look at me. I got into an American graduate school with my Filipino English."

She groaned. "But I'm not you."

Evangeline nodded, and in her silence she seemed to give Cathy her half-hearted assent. But then Evangeline said, "I'll edit you. Send your essays to me." She met Cathy's stunned gaze with a reassuring look. "You could always write travel articles. If I were you, I'd take advantage of those free trips. And then you could send me your drafts, and I could line edit them." Evangeline placed a feta cheese-powdered leaf in her mouth and chewed.

After a few seconds of silence, Evangeline swallowed and said, "Oh, come on, don't be offended. Everyone knows you're the better writer. You just said that Americans don't like our English. Sometimes it's just a question of nuance."

"And you're the expert on nuance."

"Well, I got into grad school here. Maybe they thought I could learn something."

"Vangie, you're making me want to get drunk."

Evangeline smiled. "Is that the real reason you came here?"

"You just read my mind. I have to get drunk. Dead drunk."

"Plastered, you mean?"

Cathy sighed. "Yeah, whatever. And you have to get drunk with me too."

A look of nervousness passed over Evangeline's face, and it amused Cathy to see her façade of calm goodness crumble. Cathy put her hand over Evangeline and said, "Don't worry, I'll watch out for you. You have to trust me."

"After tonight you're gonna thank me for not having a car."

"*Tama.*"

As Evangeline ran water over the dirty dishes and pots, Cathy took out the dresses she had brought and draped them on Evangeline's futon. Apparently it wasn't too difficult for her to gain the upper hand. While there were things that Evangeline was better at doing, there were things she had yet to learn, and to turn her into a willing pupil Cathy would first have to expose her ignorance.

"I'm glad you came. I've been feeling lonely ever since I arrived here," Evangeline said.

"Don't you have friends here?" Cathy asked, staring at her dresses, wondering which one her friend was willing to wear.

"I get along well with my classmates, but you know how white people are. They're more comfy when dealing with their own kind."

"You mean most of your classmates are white?"

"You could say that."

"Now that would make me very uncomfortable."

"Don't you work with white people?"

"Just white passengers, and they can be so stuck-up sometimes." Cathy picked up the fuchsia and black striped tube dress from its sleeves, and carried it to the dining area where she turned to face Evangeline. "Now, what do you think of this?" Cathy asked, draping it on her chest.

Evangeline stared at it at said, "Very daring. Very Latin."

"You're wearing it," Cathy said, and threw it at Evangeline. Evangeline was too surprised to let it fall to the floor and, after catching it, she held it before her, her face registering a faint disgust.

"We're probably the same size. I have another dress on the futon if you don't like that one."

Evangeline walked to the living room and raised an eyebrow when she saw the neon green one-shoulder dress spread on her futon like a mislaid piece of merchandise. "I can't wear that one either," she said.

"Unless you have something better to wear."

Evangeline lowered her eyes, and it dawned on Cathy that it wasn't modesty that made Evangeline hesitate. Cathy had bought both dresses at Ross, the only place where it didn't pain her to part with her money, and the brightness of these dresses now flashed at her embarrassingly. They had both been brave choices, but her bravery could have been a result of her carelessness or her simple lack of taste.

She covered up her embarrassment with a laugh and said, "Oh, come on. This isn't the Philippines. No one's gonna go after you for being slutty." She knew Evangeline was embarrassed to admit to her own lack of experience in these matters, and Evangeline giggled.

"Oh, what the hell. This means I'll really have to get drunk." Evangeline withdrew to her bedroom, draping the fuchsia and black tube dress on her arm.

She chose to ignore the hint of disappointment in Evangeline's voice, taking solace in her prediction that she'd outshine Evangeline later that night. "I'll do your makeup too," Cathy yelled with relish. "After all, you said you'd edit me!"

This wasn't Cathy's town, and she stood out in the bar-going crowd of Sixth Street; the faces of the doormen lit up when they saw her, as though hungry for variety after watching blonde after blonde walk past them. When she flashed them her California driver's license, they'd joke about knowing that she wasn't "from around these parts" as they offered her a crooked arm that she gladly took and escorted her into their music-filled bars. Evangeline trailed behind her, taking her Texas ID card from her clutch purse and returning the doormen's patronizing smiles.

"Oh my God, I think the drummer just gave me the eye," Cathy said as they carried their drinks to a table near the stage.

"How do you notice all these things?" Evangeline yelled above the music.

"You don't go out a lot, do you?" Cathy yelled back, stirring her chocolate whiskey.

She felt hungry after they had visited four bars, and they found a Mexican restaurant after walking down several blocks. After they had settled into their leatherette seats and given the waitress their orders, Cathy watched her friend from across the table. Evangeline radiated a carefree, alcoholic energy from her seat, and she leaned forward, blinking and laughing before she spoke.

"There's this guy I met. His name's David," Evangeline said.

"And he's making you all giggly," Cathy said, nodding at the waitress as a bowl of chips and salsa was set before them.

"I know. He's not my type, but I'm beginning to like him."

"Sounds promising." She pulled a chip from the pile, dipped it in salsa, and popped it in her mouth, giving Cathy a mute, prodding look.

"A classmate introduced us at a party. He's a PhD student in anthropology."

"Wow," Cathy said, her mouth full. Swallowing, she said, "At least you get to meet smart guys here. That's what I miss about college, you know? Talking to people about books, meeting smart guys."

"Hello, you could always go back to school here. You'd qualify for federal aid."

Cathy smirked. "I don't know. I'm too lazy to go back to school."

"I don't believe you," Evangeline said, drunkenly slapping the air between them with her palm. "You with your *cum laude*."

Cathy rolled her eyes. "I didn't work for that. Besides, all the forced writing we did in college made me want to quit school for good."

"Forced or not, you were good at it."

Service at this restaurant was quick, she noted. A plate of quesadillas was placed in front of her, and Evangeline stared in horror at her brownie *a la mode*.

"The newspapers I applied to didn't think so." She picked up her fork and knife and sliced off a neat corner from her quesadilla. She put it in her mouth and munched evasively.

"But you could still write while doing your airport gig. Maintain a blog or something."

"Yeah. And then you'd edit me." Cathy stared at the abundance of food on her plate, wondering why no one else in this country seemed to take notice of this habitual overindulgence. Food was so plentiful in this country one didn't have to strive for anything else.

"This is a lot of brownie," Evangeline said.

"You're still not used to the portions here?" Cathy asked.

"How can I be? They always serve us too much

food."

"You say that because you're used to eating much less."

"But this is too much."

"I said it's too much for you because you're used to eating much less." She liked the pathetic look on Evangeline's face and how much it seemed like an admission of cluelessness.

"Come on, eat up. You look like a hungry African child. And tell me more about David."

Evangeline laughed and dipped her spoon into the scoop of vanilla ice cream. "Well, he's a blond, blue-eyed Texan who's writing a dissertation about Indian culture. He has an adorable drawl. He's really smart, too."

"So, he's a white guy."

"Yeah." Evangeline paused and gave Cathy a doubtful look. "Do you have some beef with white guys?"

Cathy pursed her lips, then said, "Not really. It's just that I've never dated a white guy."

Evangeline was incredulous. "You mean out of all the guys you told me about over the phone and on Facebook—"

"The guys I've dated so far are either coworkers or friends of coworkers, and none of those people are white." She flipped through the laminated beverage list on their table. "But I'm okay with that. Latinos and black guys are great in bed." She ran her fingers through her hair, giggled, and said, "Did I tell you yet about the guy I'm sleeping with right now? Well, you've probably heard by now the myth about black guys and their, well, size. It's true, for this guy at least. And his endurance, my God! It chafes after a while, you know!"

Evangeline smiled.

"You, girl, have to go on birth control soon. As in soon. Because that white boy of yours is gonna ask for it soon."

Evangeline dug into her brownie. "He already did. But I told him I'm not ready."

"That's not the only thing you should be worried about. White guys suck in bed."

Evangeline narrowed her eyes. "How do you know that?"

"You'll know when you sleep with your white boy."

If Cathy could ever convince herself to write a story about that night, she'd probably mention how she took Evangeline home after her friend had nearly passed out on the sidewalk in front of the fifth bar they had gone to; she'd admit that she had known that Evangeline wasn't used to marathon drinking, but that Evangeline didn't seem to mind. Maybe she'd describe how Evangeline's laughter buzzed in her ears like flies' wings, and how she watched the lights of downtown Austin illuminate the interior of their cab with its indulgent, wasteful glow. Evangeline had sobered up when they had gotten home, and they helped each other fold out her futon, laughing when they realized that they couldn't figure out how they had done it when the futon finally gave in to their pushing. If words fractured a friendship, alcohol healed it, and she wished it were possible to drown in the amber-colored recklessness of that night forever.

But with sunrise came the unwanted resurfacing of the mind, and she awakened to a bright throbbing in her head and a dismal awareness of her surroundings. As she turned, her sheets rustled; she hadn't remembered Evangeline spreading these sheets, and the detailed attentiveness of her friend vexed her as her eyes fell on the drawn blinds of the living room window. The sputtering of cooking oil and the smell of brewed coffee and fried eggs reminded her of the calm domesticity that Evangeline was apt to return to after what was probably, for her, a temporary relapse. Cathy wanted to remain in bed the entire day and felt too conscious of how the rhythm of her body was out of sync with the rhythm of her surroundings. She sat up and glanced at the clock near the kitchen. It was nine in the morning.

Evangeline peeked at her from behind the kitchen wall. "Did I wake you up?" she asked.

"You did," Cathy grumbled, scratching her head.

Evangeline laughed. "I just got hungry so I made coffee and fried eggs. I made some for you too in case you woke up."

Cathy stretched and smiled. "Oh, I don't eat breakfast."

Evangeline politely raised a hand and rushed back to the kitchen. "Sorry, the eggs might burn. My God, Kat. I'd faint if I didn't have breakfast," she said from behind the wall. "Besides, we have a long day ahead of us. You'll need the energy for walking."

"Right. We're going to walk," Cathy moaned, getting up and walking to the bathroom.

Her head continued to throb as they walked around the university, and when they passed the bell tower on which the words *Ye shall know the truth and the truth shall set you free* were inscribed, she remembered that she had left her camera in California. She hadn't taken pictures ever since she had arrived, and there would be no evidence of her trip here aside from a few lingering memories that would probably disappear under the pile of worries and drunken nights in the strange cities she'd visit after this trip. For what was worth remembering in Austin? All she wanted to take with her was the freedom she felt the night before when music and lights swelled around her, eliminating the need for conversation. She complained about the heat and the dust and fanned herself furiously with her baseball cap when Evangeline tried to appease her by pointing at a statue or an empty expanse of grass. Her surroundings did not pull her in the way the bars of Austin did. In the clear light of day, these stucco buildings impressed her with their aloofness, and Evangeline's familiarity with these surroundings spoke of a sense of entitlement she could afford to be gleefully oblivious to.

"The travel guide mentions a Zilker Park and Barton Springs. Do we get to see those places too?" Cathy asked as they crossed another drearily bright avenue of paved walks and fenced-in islands of shrubbery.

"Miss, you fly back to San Francisco this afternoon. We don't have enough time, and I don't have a car to drive you around."

"I totally forgot about that."

Evangeline had a weary look on her face when she paused and turned to look at Cathy.

"Thanks for reminding me."

"Gosh, how touchy you are."

"Kat, I'm trying my best."

Cathy held both her hands up in mock surrender and said, "Okay, fine, whatever. Take me wherever you can take me."

They had lunch at a pizza parlor near campus, and afterwards they waited for a bus that would take them downtown. After ten minutes of waiting and fanning herself, she said, "If you had a car, we wouldn't be waiting this long."

"If you had rented a car, you wouldn't be waiting this long," Evangeline shot back.

A bearded, red-faced man sat at the foot of a traffic sign clutching a heavy, battered knapsack to his chest, pulling the collar of his filthy hoodie to his chin as though to take shelter inside his own clothing. Upon catching Cathy's eye, he smiled and whistled. It wasn't just his scruffiness that frightened her, but also the cheeriness with which he immersed himself in his own stench while singling her out. Why was it so difficult in this country to snuff out desire in men who had nothing?

Cathy looked away and folded her arms across her chest, eyeing the cars that sped past her, envious of the distances they could go. A grackle swooped down on her, opening its pointed beak to release a crackling screech, and she ducked and screamed. The red-faced man cackled, asked for change.

A blue metro bus finally came into view, and when its door swung open Evangeline brushed past her as she boarded the platform, inserted a few bills, collected their tickets, and handed one to Cathy without saying a word. Cathy followed Evangeline into the bus, and Evangeline turned her head away as Cathy planted herself in the seat beside her. Nothing Cathy did, it seemed, could bruise Evangeline's calculated calm – even her anger was performed with care, as though she had practiced these gestures before in the event of a quarrel. Cathy knew that what Evangeline wanted from her was an apology, but this was

something Cathy wouldn't give to her that easily. If Cathy were to be honest with herself, she'd admit that it was an apology from Evangeline that would quell her own anger – an apology for accepting this shoddy life and forcing it upon her.

Cathy gazed above Evangeline's head at the scenes that rolled past her like pictures in a View Master toy. She wanted to see something different in this town, something that would astonish her. Although the dome of the State Capitol Building impressed her with its rosy massiveness, many of the things she saw were familiar to her: the churches, the parking garages, the chain restaurants of the downtown area, the abundance of cars on the road. This was all Evangeline was capable of showing her in this musty-smelling bus. Evangeline's spartan lifestyle reminded Cathy of her own shoddy apartment and the cheap clothes she was forced to wear, and she was exasperated by the way in which Evangeline compensated for her present poverty with an optimism that Cathy didn't share. Evangeline was convinced she knew where her life was going – she had told Cathy that her dream was to be an academic, and Cathy imagined her surrounding herself with people who shared her naïveté of the world at large. It was these people who could afford to snub the modest American Dream of material comforts, a dream that was less delusional and easier for Cathy to embrace. It required little from her aside from optimism in the freedoms she already had.

> **" But then she had to touch the ground in cities that were beginning to look increasingly alike. "**

There was one desire she found easy to fulfill in this sprawling country, and it was the weightlessness she felt as she traveled across America by plane. But then she had to touch the ground in cities that were beginning to look increasingly alike, whose scrubbed cleanliness only served to remind her of the closer affinities she shared with the polluted, monsoon-drenched streets of Manila.

"I'm sorry if I can't drive you around," Evangeline said in a hard, sarcastic voice.

"There's nothing we can do about it," Cathy said, feeling the dryness of her throat.

When they had crossed a bridge and reached an eclectic row of one-storey shops, Evangeline pulled the window string beside her and Cathy stepped aside and followed her lead as they got off the bus. She took Cathy to a curiosity shop called Uncommon Objects, and Cathy noticed the abundance of doll heads and framed photographs of white, blushing babies. She looked at their price tags and gasped at the quoted figures.

"You can just imagine how much money we'd make if we raided our houses back in the Philippines and sold off all the worthless junk our grandmothers kept," she said.

"Nobody sells their heirlooms back home. Family property is family property," Evangeline said, staring at a Victorian baby doll in a mottled gingham dress.

"Imagine how creepy it would be if that white baby stared at me from my wall," Cathy said, pointing at another baby picture.

"Pretend she was your daughter in your past life. Maybe that would help."

Cathy grinned. "If I could get away with it," she said between her teeth.

In another corner of the store, a narrow-waisted, Victorian-style lace dress hung inside an open wooden closet, and Cathy stood on tiptoe as she took it down. She draped the bust over her chest, allowing the skirt to brush the floor. "I'd love to wear this for Halloween, but I'm too short. The skirt would drag behind me."

"It'd *trail* behind you, not *drag* behind you." There was a slight, mocking lilt in Evangeline's voice, and she raised an eyebrow.

"Whatever," Cathy said, returning the dress to the closet. She turned and made her way to the door without waiting for Evangeline to catch up.

"You're the one doing the dragging, not the skirt," Evangeline said, following Cathy through the aisles of the store.

As Cathy pushed the glass door open with her side, she took out her cellphone, logged onto Yelp, and when she caught a signal, checked in to the store.

"What were you doing that for?" Evangeline asked when they had stepped outside.

"Just checking in to this store on Yelp," Cathy said. "It's too weird not to be reviewed by me."

"You write Yelp reviews?" Evangeline asked, amused.

"It's my new hobby." She slipped her cellphone into her faux leather purse and, with a quick, purposeful gesture, zipped her purse shut. They walked down the street, and when Evangeline spotted a bookstore, she pulled open the glass door and held it as Cathy entered.

Evangeline seemed to know what she wanted for she gravitated immediately towards a bookcase near the shop window, pulling out books written by Susan Sontag, Michel Foucault, French philosophers who wrote in a style that seemed, when Cathy had been in college with Evangeline, to be intentionally hermetic.

The tactfulness with which Evangeline kept mum about the books she'd read or the ideas she had encountered was, for Cathy, vaguely condescending. Cathy wandered around the bookstore, reading blurbs of graphic novels, avoiding the thick, hardbound books, ambassadors of a lost era when readers like she weren't too impatient to bypass the challenge of a prolonged read, when they could impose upon themselves a stasis that promised few rewards.

As she stood before a bookshelf near the back of the store looking at a softbound copy of *The Great Gatsby*, Evangeline sneaked behind her. "And who reads these Yelp reviews?" Evangeline asked, her sarcasm couched in her sickly-sweet voice.

"People who could use my opinions about these stores," she said. "At least there's some use in what I write." She looked at the cover of the book Evangeline was clutching to her chest and said, "Not everyone's smart enough to waste their time reading useless Lacanian theories."

Evangeline smiled. "If you put your intelligence to good use a little more, you wouldn't be stuck writing Yelp reviews."

"I'm intelligent enough to know what's useful," Cathy said, brushing past her and making her way to the shop's front door.

She hadn't realized until she had stepped into the fresh outdoor air that she needed Evangeline to find her way back to the apartment where she had left her things. She wished she had predicted this moment so that she could have left Evangeline's apartment with all her things on her back, but how could one be capable of preparing for disorder when it was in one's nature to create it? She watched Evangeline through the window of the store, paying for the book she had found, smiling at the cashier as she received her change. It was impossible to knock down the windowpane that separated the two of them without hurting Evangeline. She was hurt, Cathy could tell. Evangeline pushed the shop door open, clutching her bagged purchase, and gave Cathy an icy look. A group of women twice their size in combat boots and baby doll dresses passed between the two of them. If Cathy looked just like them, she could've merged with their pack instead of confronting the anger of the person who was, in this town, her single friend.

"We're going home," Evangeline said, pointing at the bus stop on the other side of the road.

Back in the apartment, Evangeline called a cab service as Cathy packed her bag, and when her taxi arrived, Evangeline gave her a final, perfunctory hug. "I'm sorry if I was rude to you. We're still friends, aren't we?"

"Of course." In America, the word *friend* meant anything.

"I wish you happiness in whatever you choose to

do. I'm not bullshitting, Kat. I mean it."

"Thanks for the sincerity," Cathy said, breaking away from Evangeline's stiff embrace.

If this scene were taking place in Manila, she would've been walking towards her cab amidst car honks, wailing babies, lines of dripping laundry, and the footsteps and laughter of passersby. In their homeland, there were too many noises, smells, and sights to distract them from the silence of inevitable partings. It took a trip to America for them to realize that they had parted long ago.

On the plane back to San Francisco, she closed her eyes as the ground released her into the weight-lessness of the Austin sky. There was no need for her to look out the window – she had seen it all and sought only release from the heaviness she had begun to feel when she parted with Evangeline. It used to be that she brought a notebook with her whenever she went on a trip so that she could unburden herself on paper during long flights such as these. But in her effort to travel light, she discarded the things she had no use for, and after a few more trips, her notebook, like many of her previous necessities, had lost its use. Maybe it was this weightless-ness of mind that she truly wanted, for only indifference could truly extinguish her longing. She'd have to will this indifference for now. Sooner or later, it would come to her naturally. She'd be like a bird taking flight.

MELATONIN DREAMS
& THE ENDING OF WINTER

Francis Daulerio

I am remembering tonight
what happiness feels like –

    bare feet
    tracking black mulch across
    the hardwood foyer,

    the way little white flowers
    my wife calls starlight
    bloom sideways
    out of the quiet walls of the creek,
    swaying in the wind above
    shallow water
    crawling over swollen firewood
    tossed in, those drunken nights
    warmed then only by the closeness
    of our bodies,

    and my heart,
    slowly regaining itself,
    pacing with the cadence
    of the small green frogs,
    a call bouncing out of mud,
        answered somewhere farther off
        in the early darkness
        of morning.

IN A CHAPEL BUILT OF TREES

Robert James Russell *Previously published in (b)OINK*

Yes, we had a fight in the logging camp bunkhouse re-creation diorama. Yes, we did! You were looking at an old photographic print glued onto particle board – scratched, faded from greasy fingerprints – of a logging camp group shot. We had been fighting about your brother, I think. He wanted to homeschool, and you – Wait, hear me out! – were all for it, and I, yes, had some things to say about that. But, nevertheless, inside the cramped reconstruction while looking at the tiny bunks, wondering if I'd be able to fit on them myself – if, somehow, I'd found myself traveled back through time, how I'd ever get a good night's rest on one of these beds, and that, surely, a good night's rest is mandatory for the physically exhausting labor of being a logger, right? – we swallowed our pride and said we'd talk about it later on the drive home.

You waved me back over then. You said, "Come look at this old photograph."

I said, "It's not old. They probably printed that like ten years ago."

"Print," you said. "This old print. Whatever, you know what I mean. Quit being a shit."

I was being a shit, and I was aware of it, too, so I joined you at your side. You pointed to the figures, waved your hands across the photograph – framed in cheesy orange-red glazed wood paneling – as if presenting a school project. I squinted: the photograph was taken in the winter. Two bunkhouses, a re-creation of which we were standing in, were encased in snow. Stacks of lumber stood in front (also covered in white), massive trunks of red and white pine felled and awaiting dissection.

Wasn't there a term for stacks of logs like this, I thought? I had just read it on one of the other boards, I was sure. I almost asked you.

Back to the photo, then: About thirty people, men and women, a child, too, sitting on one of the felled trees, all staring at the photographer blankly. I said, "These photos always weird me out."

"Why?"

"They're always so serious, you know? It's like they're transfixed. Even the horses. Look." I pointed to a team of horses off to the side that, yes, like the others, were staring impassively at the camera. "Had they never really seen a camera before?" I touched the print, ran my index finger along some of the faces – all white and impossibly unblemished like the snow. Behind them, deep in the background, the same red

and white pine surrounding us and this logging village museum – yet many decades before this park, Hartwick Pines State Park, the third largest state park in the lower peninsula, was established.

And that's what drew us there: the old growth forest, preserved pines estimated to be between 350 and 375 years old. Massive-trunked trees – some with girths of more than four feet, even! – a forest of them, untouched by man. You and I were always drawn to places like that, the serenity of those ancient landscapes. We had wandered in, gasped aloud to one another, "What was the world even like when these trees were saplings?" and stood in awe of them. The trails were quiet and we were alone. At one point, I wedged myself into the cavity of a dead jack pine, tried to make you laugh.

"Look!" I said. "I can barely fit! Want to take a picture?"

You smiled, you did – for a moment – but then you shook your head. "You lied to me."

"I didn't lie."

"You told me you always wanted a family." You paused. "Two kids, you told me."

"I'm not saying I don't. I just...in *this* world? Really?"

"The world's always been shitty," you said. You took a deep breath. You said, "What makes us special to say no way?"

"I don't want to make the mistakes of my parents. You know that. I dread that."

"But you're not them. And you have me by your side."

"But people with kids drift apart. I like what we have now."

"They don't always."

"Most do."

"My brother and his wife didn't."

And...we know where this went, right? How we got to talking about his homeschooling, how we changed topics, deflected – how we decided, in the interest of preserving the peace of the park, that we better just let it be. So we continued on in agonizing silence along the trail. There was no wind, no sounds of birds or squirrels or chipmunks. We felt miniaturized – well, at least I did – walking by these trees, spread out, standing at their bases, looking up to the sky, how they umbrellaed out and hid the sun from us, the land below some ghostly other plane.

You sighed, and we removed ourselves slowly from the bunkhouse, back to the trail. We walked another quarter mile – still in silence, although I wanted to talk to you, I wanted to make it right, but I didn't know how. Around the bend we saw a structure, what we thought at first was a small A-frame log cabin, another reconstruction. But we realized, as we got closer, it was a chapel. The steeple was small, stunted. We wondered how long it had been here. Then, remember, we heard voices as we approached.

At the front door, two park rangers were sweeping up the entrance, mumbling to one another. "Sorry," one of them said to us. "Let's get out of your way here."

Inside the chapel it was pitch-black, but at the far wall, we were marveled: a cross cut into the timbers – a chunky, massive cross, window-paned and looking out into the brush. Outside, beyond it, more of the virgin white and red pine, tamarack and jack pine. So when you looked at the cross-shaped window, all you saw was nature, this park.

You wandered up to the front to touch the glass. I took a seat in the back pew, watching. I remembered, then, back when I believed in churches, in that god. I remembered Sunday School and church dinners and all the people I spent years with who were no longer a part of my life. Except you. I remember meeting you there, our collective joy in asking our Sunday School teachers impossible questions about dinosaurs and ancient things, asking for timetables – why were there no exact timetables in the Bible? Oh, how we delighted in flustering them!

Then I snickered aloud, laughed.

You turned and said to me, "What?"

"It's just funny to me, a chapel out here. Like these woods, this place, isn't worthy itself to be praised."

"People like their churches. You know that."

"Yeah, I know."

You put your hand back on the glass, and you started to hum – you do that, you know, when you're inspired or anxious or when you don't want silence when there should be words.

"What changed?" you said to me, but didn't turn around.

I didn't answer you. I still couldn't, I don't think. Or, how about this: Time changed. We met, what, junior year of high school? We escaped our families, those parts of our lives we had wanted altered and improved upon – escaped into one another. So, these trails and these hikes, these explorations of wild areas, it all made sense, you know? We made a list, we both had a copy with cute notes and doodles in the margins, and we scratched off these state and national parks as we visited them, as we questioned their formations, studied their flora.

And, yes, we talked about children all through the rest of high school because all couples do that, right?

And in college, sure, we kept it up because that was the future. It was something to look toward. Another thing to cross off our list. We had names picked out and everything. At your cousin's wedding, after we graduated, right after you took that job and were on such a high – at the reception when you zany danced with your nieces and nephews – you hugged me after and told me you couldn't wait to have our own someday. If I could pinpoint it, I guess that was the first time I really think I felt something different. But you know what I did? I smiled and said, "Sure, of course. I love it. I love you."

But all these years later, I remember this, the last road trip, the last state park (although we didn't know it then). There, in the chapel darkness, the only light coming through the cross-shaped window, how I sat uncomfortably in that back wooden pew. I watched you. I wondered what our talk later on the hours-long drive home would be like. I studied your silhouette, your hair tied back, your long, slender legs. I touched my chest, balled my hand up in a fist there. Then I looked past you through the cross cut into the timbers, past you to the trees, the woods. It was all I could see.

OCEANIC

Nick Alti

A warning, a shout from the forest – forget the lake
where singing dissipates;

the drowned want you sunk.
Me think, well, me thinking I go about
in a deluge, a delirium/sybaritic tremens
not very less painful than a selenic implosion
but certainly with less effect on gravity as a whole.

I'm trying to say I see you always in turbulence.
It's the universe telling us we need time apart;   lacuna   fermata.

*

Take a picture of Lake Erie & bathe with it,
bathe in it,
bathe in your new tenderness; I'll take your leftover watercolors
& mix it with blood from the woodchuck
your father trapped last August.

All of this to say conversation with you anymore is a sad thunder.
Maybe, in a while, we can be pen pals.
(While waiting I've forged a letter to a prisoner
asking for a drawing of an abstract corpse in response. I signed it *Mother dearest.*)

*

We never figured out your great fear of water.
Page two of my book misses being a tree.
It's a tome of potential titles for an essay I'll write on understanding water, or anything within it.
   - A Galaxy of Fish
   - The Fish is the Galaxy
   - River Fishing in Beirut
   - Is There an Actual Difference Between a Fish & Myself as a Grown Man Hiding in the Closet?
   - fuckfishshitwater
   - I'm So Sick of Fish
   - Why Did You Move to an Island

It isn't a good book. I'd rather have
a tree,
either outside
or growing out of my ribcage
blossoming elderberries
for fish to eat.

CURING

Francis Daulerio

In two months' time
the garlic leaves
will brown
and we will dig papery bulbs
from cedar darkness,
twisting them like widows' braids
to swing from the attic beam above
my dead grandfather's sawhorses.

In two months' time
my daughter will take wobbly steps,
an unripe tomato gripped tight
between her chubby fingers,
toward the June bug trap
we've warned her
away from again and again
with exaggerated eyebrows,
playfully stern.

In two months' time
I will look behind me,
shocked at my distance,
eyes to the creek rushing
storm water west,
and say something quiet,
mostly to myself,
about how fast it all goes
or how I'm scared to go to sleep,
        each new dawn receding so quickly
            back to sunset.

Contributors

ELISABETH ALAIN lives in Worcestershire, raising two daughters and writing short stories and poetry. Her work has appeared in the print anthology *Please Hear What I'm Not Saying* and online in *The Cabinet of Heed*, *Paragraph Planet*, *The Drabble*, *Dear Damsels*, *The Ginger Collect*, and *Black Country Arts Foundry*.

FRANCIS DAULERIO is a writer, teacher, and author of two collaborative collections of poetry and art. His 2015 debut, *If & When We Wake*, chronicles the process of healing after loss. His newest collection, a 50th-anniversary reinterpretation of Richard Brautigan's *Please Plant This Book*, benefits the American Foundation for Suicide Prevention. Kaveh Akbar has called his work "staggering, gorgeous, essential." Francis lives outside of Philadelphia with his wife, daughter, and a small herd of deer. More information can be found at FRANCISDAULERIO.COM.

HALEY CAMPBELL is a writer and editor living in Austin, Texas. She received her BA in English from the University of Mary Washington and writes about bodies, chronic pain, queerness, and love. You can find her on Twitter @HALEY_EXE or at HALEYCAMPBELL.NET. These are her first published pieces.

JENNIFER FLISS is a Seattle-based fiction and essay writer. Her work has appeared in *PANK*, *Hobart*, *The Rumpus*, *Gigantic Sequins*, and elsewhere. She can be found on Twitter at @WRITESFORLIFE or via her website, WWW.JENNIFERFLISSCREATIVE.COM.

KATHRYN LIPARI reads and writes in Portland, Oregon. Her short fiction has appeared in journals including *Smokelong Quarterly*, *Typehouse Ink*, *Marathon Literary Review*, and *Women's Studies Quarterly*. She is a member of Full Frontal Writing Collective and smallSalon.com. When not writing she might be found running the city's muddy trails or hectoring her three imaginative kids.

KRISTEN M. PLOETZ is a writer and former attorney living in Massachusetts. Her recent short fiction has been published (or is forthcoming) with *FIVE:2:ONE*, *jmww*, *Gravel*, *Hypertext Magazine*, *Lost Balloon*, *The Hopper*, *Maudlin House*, and elsewhere. She is currently working on a YA novel and a collection of short stories. You can find her on the web at WWW.KRISTENPLOETZ.COM and Twitter (@KRISTENPLOETZ).

MONICA MACANSANTOS was born and raised in the Philippines and holds an MFA in writing from the Michener Center for Writers in Austin, Texas. Her work has recently appeared in *WSQ: Women's Studies Quarterly*, *Takahe*, *Willow*, and *Amazon's Day One*, among other places. Her work has received recognition from *The Best American Essays 2016* and the Glimmer Train Fiction Open. She is currently a PhD candidate in Creative Writing at Victoria University of Wellington in New Zealand where she is working on her first novel.

NICK ALTI bartends in Holland, MI. He somehow weaseled his way into The University of Alabama's MFA program starting this August. This is exciting for him, yes, but he fears there will be hurricanes, large mosquitoes, and, quite frankly, hurricanes composed of large mosquitoes. He's never been farther south than Indiana. He has a crippling fear of balloons (it's called globophobia okay it's a real thing) and recently someone tried to gun him down at a drive-through spaghetti restaurant.

ROBERT JAMES RUSSELL is the author of the novellas *Mesilla* (Dock Street Press) and *Sea of Trees* (Winter Goose Publishing), and the chapbook *Don't Ask Me to Spell It Out* (WhiskeyPaper Press). He is a founding editor of the literary journals *Midwestern Gothic* and *CHEAP POP*. You can find him online at ROBERTJAMESRUSSELL.COM.

TOMMY DEAN is the author of a flash fiction chapbook entitled *Special Like the People on TV* from Redbird Chapbooks. A graduate of the Queens University of Charlotte MFA program, he has been previously published in *The MacGuffin*, *Bull Magazine*, *Split Lip Magazine*, *JMWW*, *Hawaii Pacific Review*, and *New World Writing*. Find him @TOMMYDEANWRITER on Twitter.

VERONIKA VAJDOVA is originally from Slovakia. She is a self-taught artist who kept spending more and more time creating new art, which led to her currently studying 3D animation and visualisation in the UK. Some people pour their life into their diaries or blogs; Veronika prefers to express herself through her art. By experimenting with colors and shapes, she wants the viewer to feel compelled to stop and think about the story behind the picture and maybe even find their own story. Find her work at SOCIETY6.COM/WERONI.

Index

ELISABETH ALAIN
  Lemon Scent..10
FRANCIS DAULERIO
  Curing..41
  Melatonin Dreams & the Ending of Winter..34
  Poem for a Sick Child on the Fourth of July..21
HALEY CAMPBELL
  Field of Malachite..20
  Heritable..14
  You Said I Want..24
JENNIFER FLISS
  A Man Who Helps the Neighbors..13
  My Syllables..15
KATHRYN LIPARI
  Your Mother Has Another Black Eye and..9
KRISTEN M. PLOETZ
  Bitter Pills..21
MONICA MACANSANTOS
  Stopover..25
NICK ALTI
  Lightmare..11
  Oceanic..38
  Solitude Audible..17
ROBERT JAMES RUSSELL
  In a Chapel Built of Trees..35
TOMMY DEAN
  A Thrumming Silence..19

ART BY VERONIKA VAJDOVA
"My Pulse," digital, 2016..Front Cover
"Then I Saw It," mixed media, 2016..2
"Bye," mixed media, 2018..6, 7
"Stars from Within," mixed media, 2018..8
"Venom," digital, 2016..11
"Dream," mixed media, 2018..12
"Freedom," mixed media, 2018..14
"Enlighten Me," digital, 2016..16
"Mirror Mirror," ink, 2018..18
"Lavender Me," mixed media, 2018..21
"Sunshine," mixed media, 2018..22
"Farba," digital, 2016..24
"In Progress," digital, 2018..33
"They See," mixed media, 2018..34
"Together," mixed media, 2018..37
"Cacti," digital, 2017..39
"Metamorphosis," digital, 2017..40, 41

DO NOT LET YOUR EYES ADJUST TO THE DARKNESS.

"STAGGERING, GORGEOUS, ESSENTIAL"
KAVEH AKBAR, AUTHOR OF *CALLING A WOLF A WOLF*

"SPARE, RELAXED, WISE, AND TRUE"
MAGGIE SMITH, AUTHOR OF *GOOD BONES*

"FRANCIS DAULERIO IS A MASTERFUL POET"
GREGORY ALAN ISAKOV

A 50th anniversary reinterpretation of Richard Brautigan's 1968 seed project
featuring poetry and art by Francis Daulerio and Scott Hutchison.
All proceeds benefit the American Foundation For Suicide Prevention.

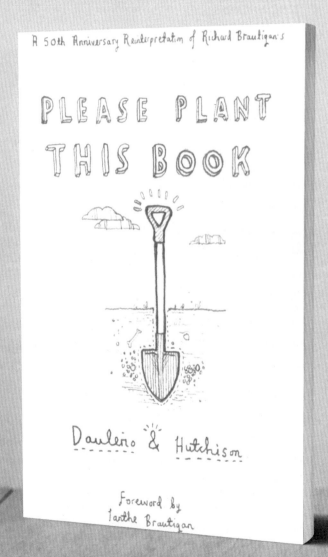

She Used to Be on a Milk Carton

A Debut Collection of Poetry
by Kailey Tedesco

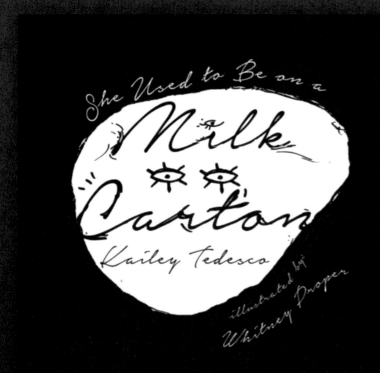

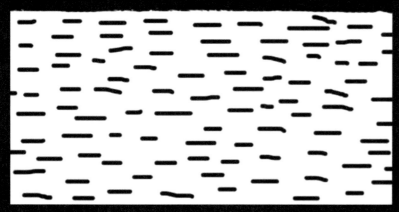

"If you have ever pretended to be Lydia from Beetlejuice or enjoy visiting catacombs on vacation, you'll love this book!"
- Genevieve Betts,
Author of An Unwalled City

"…a decadent, mesmeric, dangerous collection."
- Jessie Janeshek
Author of The Shaky Phase

"…these poems will challenge your emotional status quo, but most definitely, in all the ways that will make the heart inside your chest beat like a drum."
- Michelle Reale,
Author of Birds of Sicily

"Kailey Tedesco's poetry builds haunted Victorian dollhouses in the eternal moment where childish innocence collides with grown-up wickedness."
- Joseph P. Obrien,
Managing Editor of
FLAPPERHOUSE

Out now from April Gloaming Publishing
Available at Amazon.com and through select book sellers.

For more information about the author, visit kaileytedesco.com

Made in the USA
San Bernardino, CA
09 June 2018